Nature at Work

Contents | Page

written by Jack Gabolinscy

Forces of nature are at work. They are very strong, and they never stop. We can see and feel their power.

rainbow

The Sun is a strong force of nature.
It makes night and day on Earth.

As Earth spins, the side facing the Sun is in daylight. The side that faces away from the Sun is nighttime.

Sunlight warms Earth and makes plants grow. It keeps the world alive.

If there was no Sun, there would be no plants on the land or in the sea.

The wind is moving air. Sunlight is a force of energy that makes the winds blow. The Sun warms the air and makes it move.

Wind can become stronger
and blow much harder.

Some forces of nature work from underground. A volcano starts from deep inside Earth, where there is red-hot melted rock.

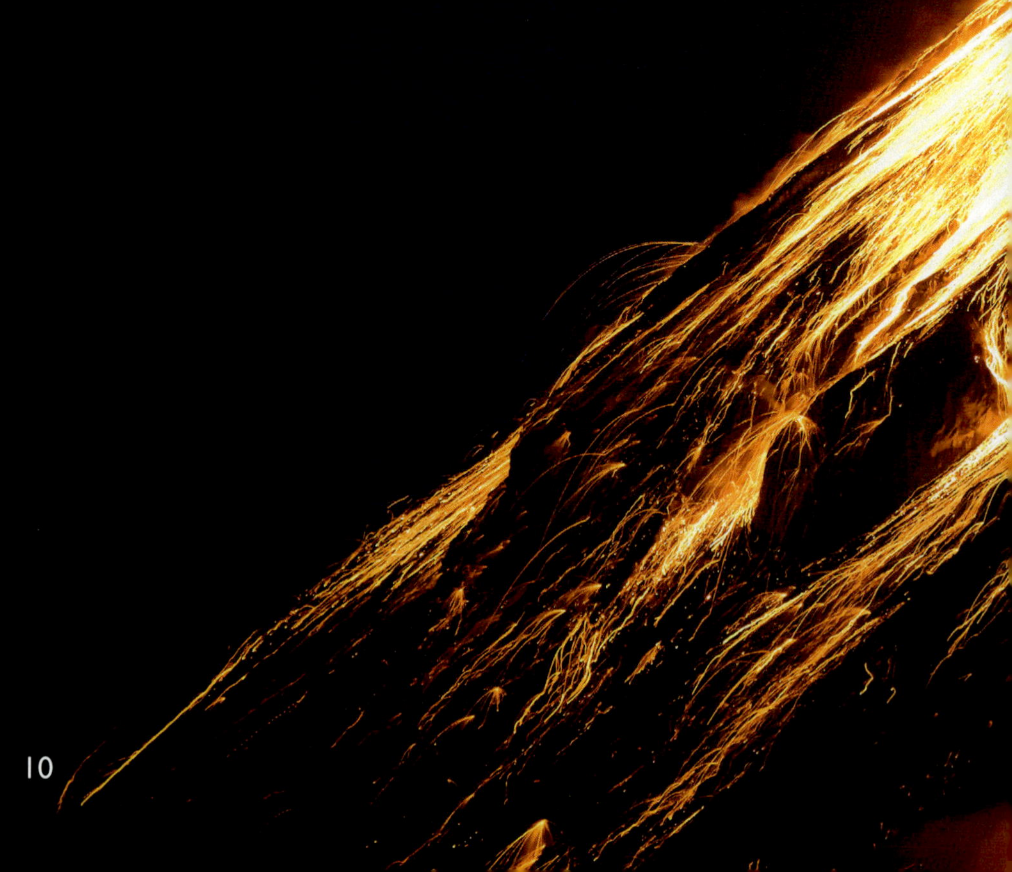

The red-hot rock pushes up through cracks under the volcano. It erupts, with gas, lava, ash, and steam flying into the air. Rivers of red-hot lava run down the sides of the volcano.

An earthquake is a force of nature that happens when Earth's surface moves. A small earthquake shakes houses and makes things rattle.

A strong earthquake can knock down big things.

Gravity holds things down. It makes the rain fall. The Sun's gravity keeps Earth and other planets moving.

The pull of Earth's gravity keeps the Moon turning. The Moon has gravity, too, but it is not as strong as Earth's gravity.

Nothing can stop nature at work. Forces of nature will keep working forever, changing the world.